# THEOLOGY
# of the Body
## some thoughts & reflections

KAREN DOYLE

Theology of the Body, some thoughts and reflections.
First published 2008.

Karen Doyle.
ISBN 978-0-9775315-8-5

Graphic Design by Jeanine Doyle.
Photography by Jonathan Doyle.

Printed by Brougham Press, Melbourne.
Published by CHOICEZ MEDIA
GPO BOX14 Canberra City ACT 2601

# *Dedication*

To my parents who gave me the greatest gift of all, my life.

Thank you for all the sacrifices you made, the love you showed and the sincere gift of self that you made to each other and to your children.

It is really now, as an adult and parent, that I realize how much you gave. Thank you.

# Introduction

Throughout history, human beings have always asked fundamental questions about life and destiny, such as "Who am I? What is the meaning and purpose of my existence? And how do I find true and lasting fulfillment?" Modern culture attempts to answer these questions very glibly by promoting, for example, personal sexual pleasure as the primary goal of human existence and confusing a desire for sex with our yearning for intimacy. The tragedy of this perception is that after fleeting sexual encounters, people often find themselves feeling hurt and increasingly unfulfilled.

In contrast to the manner in which modern culture attempts to answer these questions of the heart, the real answer actually lies upon the path of understanding the significance of our bodies, as male and female, and how the physical, embodied reality of our gender reveals spiritual truths about God and the meaning of life.

These spiritual truths were explored in great depth by Pope John Paul II over a period of four years during which he dedicated his weekly General Audience to investigating these questions. This body of work is known as *The Theology of the Body*. It has been described by George Weigel, the papal autobiographer as a *"theological time bomb set to go off, with dramatic consequences, sometime in the third millennium of the Church."*

Building on spiritual tradition, Pope John Paul II makes a significant contribution to the Church's rich understanding of the human person and human sexuality. He does this through a unique examination of the significance of the *body* and how the *body* reveals something of the image and likeness of God.

Regardless of whether you are married, desiring marriage, single or celibate, I invite you to engage your heart with the truths contained in the *Theology of the Body* and I pray that your eyes and hearts would be open to the truth, beauty and goodness of the human body in light of God's original plan.

Yours in Christ

*Karen*

In the beginning

*"In the beginning* God created the heavens and the earth...

God saw what he had made, and behold, it was very good."

{Genesis 1:31}

In the beginning...

We are all too familiar with the way in which sin has perverted sex and distorted the attitudes of many to the human body. However, John Paul II has given us great hope that despite the effects of sin in the world, through Christ's redeeming love and sacrifice, it is possible for us to experience the body and human sexuality as God originally intended. This journey of healing and discovery begins and ends with Christ.

In Matthew's Gospel Jesus is questioned by the Pharisees about the indissolubility of marriage (Matt 19:3-9). When asked how it was that Moses allowed divorce Jesus answered; *"it is because of your hardness of heart that Moses allowed you to divorce...but from the beginning it was not so."* This statement *'from the beginning'* is foundational to John Paul II's *Theology of the Body.* Following the lead of Christ, he takes us back to the '*beginning'* and explores God's original plan for life, love and human happiness.

Through a comprehensive examination of the deeply symbolic nature of the Genesis narrative, John Paul II seeks to develop an 'adequate anthropology'- an understanding of the truth about what a human person truly is. In seeking to establish for us an understanding of the original experience of the body, and human sexuality prior to original sin, John Paul II develops three key original human experiences; original solitude, original unity and original nakedness, collectively termed *original innocence*. It is these experiences that reveal what it truly means to be a person and it is these experiences that we must explore and re-encounter in order to fully grasp the meaning of sex, life and human love.

# In the beginning…

God's original plan for life and love

Original solitude

Original unity

Original nakedness

Original sin

# Original Solitude

The first state is that of original solitude, in which man first discovers his personhood. In the first account of creation, 'man' refers to male and female collectively: *"God created man in his own image and likeness...male and female he created them."* (Genesis 1:27)

It is in the experience of original solitude that man becomes aware that he is unlike any of the other creatures around him. After creating the world and the creatures in it, God brings each of these to the man to name. It is in naming the creatures that man realizes there is no one like him; while he and the creatures exist in the visible world, he recognizes that he is different, that there is no one with whom he can relate as his equal. Importantly, his *body* is different.

The meaning of original solitude is twofold. Firstly, man is alone and unadorned before God, his Lord and Creator. Secondly, and crucially, he recognizes that something is missing - he desires to be in communion with another human person, another 'I'.

"Man was created with an elevated dignity to that of the other creatures. *Formed* from the dust he is a manifestation of God in the world, a sign of his presence, a trace of his glory."

{John Paul II}

*His body,* through
which he participates
in the visible created world,
makes him at the same time conscious of
being alone.

"By means of this test
(naming the creatures), man becomes
aware of his own superiority, that is,
that he cannot be considered on the same
footing as any other species of living
beings on earth."

(John Paul II)

What distinguishes man and woman from the animal
world is the
*ability to choose,*
importantly to choose to love.

*This freedom of will is given to us by God, so that we may choose to give love and receive love. It is in this way that we share in God's divine plan.*

# Original Unity

*I*n Genesis 2:28, the second account of creation, we specifically see the creation of woman as a profound overcoming of man's original solitude. God recognizes that it is not good for the man to be alone, and so creates a helpmate and companion suitable for him.

Causing the man to fall into a deep sleep, from his rib he creates woman. When the man awakes God presents the man and the woman to one another as a *gift*, one to and for the other. The man is overcome with joy and exclaims, *"at last, this is bone of my bone and flesh of my flesh."* In other words *"at last here is a person, another 'I' with whom I can relate and share my life."* While he notices that she is different from him he is profoundly aware that they share a common humanity.

The man and the woman then become *"one flesh"*, and this is the experience of original unity, in which the man finds fulfillment in relationship firstly with God and then with another.

This is not to say that without a sexual partner a person is incomplete, but rather it teaches us that as human persons we are created for relationship with others and it is in this sense that we are able to fulfill the very meaning of our existence.

"Masculinity and *femininity* are distinct,
yet at the same time they complement
and explain each other."

{John Paul II}

*"He (man) realizes it (his essence) only by
existing "with someone"
and even more deeply and completely by existing
"for someone."*

"The person becomes
*the image and likeness of God,*
not so much in the
moment of solitude but in the moment of
communion."

{John Paul II}

"God calls man,
'in his image and likeness'
to rule over the earth.
This sharing in God's lordship reaches its
highest calling in the
specific responsibility he gave man and woman,
the protection and establishment of
human life."
'in his image and likeness'

{John Paul II}

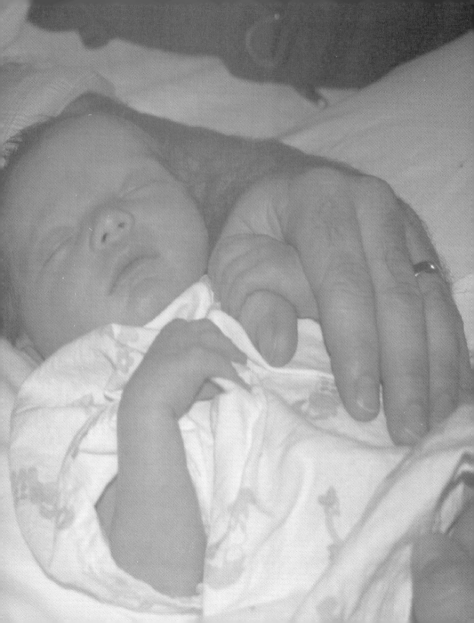

As complementary friend and helpmate, the man
and woman call each
other beyond themselves and in doing so they help
each other reach fulfillment.

*"The Man recognized and found his own humanity with the help of the woman."*

(John Paul II)

# Original Nakedness

The third original human experience, prior to sin entering the world, is that of original nakedness. It is this experience that reveals the fundamental truth and meaning about our existence as male and female and importantly, our capacity for sexual relationship. 'Original nakedness' also embraces truthful communication – in thought, word and deed. Our emotions, our thoughts and our actions are pure before God, and before one another.

In Genesis 2:25 we learn that the man and the woman were before each other and they *"were naked and they felt no shame."* Prior to sin entering the world, the man and woman were free from a desire to take sexually from one another- to exploit one another for personal sexual gratification. They also had no experience of shame as they they had no need to hide their bodies from the lustful eye of the other, because they loved with a pure love that posed no threat to the dignity of the other person. Instead, they recognized the call to love as God loves, in and through their bodies and they did this by giving themselves *freely* to one another in a relationship of mutual, self donative and reciprocal love.

The fact that they were *"naked and they felt no shame"*, specifically communicates that both the man and the woman experienced a conscious awareness of both the external and the internal significance of their own body and the body of the other, the body as a gift.

" *Nakedness* signifies the
original good of God's vision.

It signifies all the *simplicity and fullness* of the vision
through which the 'pure' value of
humanity as male and female,
the 'pure' value of the body and of sex, is manifested."

{John Paul II}

"Man and woman *communicate* on the basis of the communion of persons in which, through *femininity and masculinity,* they become a gift for each other. In this way they reach in reciprocity a special understanding of the meaning of their own body."

(John Paul II)

Designed right from the beginning, sexual desire
was intended to be the desire to love in the imago dei,
*the image of God.*

*"They (man and woman) see and
know each other with the
peace of the interior gaze,
which creates precisely the fullness of the
intimacy of persons."*

{John Paul II}

Original Sin

*I*n the beginning, God desired us to be in full communion with him and each other, filled with his love. The first man and woman had the capacity to make a *'disinterested gift of self,'* to give themselves freely and without reservation. The purity and peacefulness of God's original plan was ruptured when sin entered the world.

Sin changed their capacity, as it does ours, to make a pure gift of ourselves in love. John Paul II highlights that sin causes us to question God's gift of love. Instead of sexual desire being the power by which man and woman seek to make a gift of themselves, sin distorts our capacity to make a gift of our self in this way. Sexual desire now becomes a desire to take from and possess the other.

As Jesus points out in the Sermon on the Mount *(Matthew 5)*, the problem with lust is not a problem of the body, but rather a problem of the heart. Sin distorts man's understanding and ability to live the nuptial meaning of the body. Our nuptial existence is founded on 'giving' not taking. When the desires of our heart are disordered we are incapable of experiencing the wonder and beauty of God's original plan. But through the redeeming love of Christ's sacrifice for us on the cross we are able to overcome the lustful desires of the heart and experience the fullness of relationship with God and each other, as God intended..." *in the beginning.*"

"Instead of *being united*, they were even opposed because of their masculinity and femininity."

{John Paul II}

*Sin rejects God's gift by
breaking the original unity of man and
woman, leading to a collapse in the
communion of persons.*

"The heart has become the battleground *between love and lust.*
The more lust dominates the heart, the less
the heart experiences the nuptial
meaning of the body, it becomes less sensitive
to the gift of the person."

{John Paul II}

Create in me a *pure heart* oh Lord,
and renew a steadfast spirit within me.

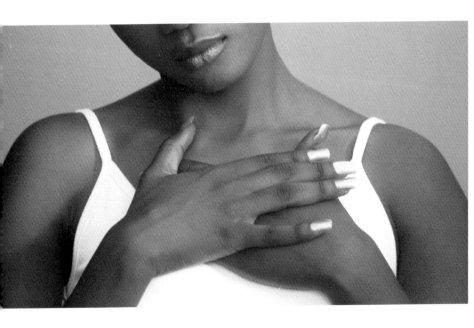

# The nuptial meaning of the body

*J*ohn Paul II places great emphasis on the significance of the human body stating that, *"it represents a value not sufficiently appreciated."*[1] This value lies in the deeply symbolic nature of the body. Rather than being simply a physical entity, the human body reveals the deepest reality of the person, the living soul. Not only does the body reveal the individual person but it is also an expression of God's very own revelation of himself. That is what is meant by a "theology of the body". We usually think of theology being the study of God but here it means that God chooses to reveal who he is and how he loves us through the bodily expression of human love and commitment. God is revealed in and through the human body.

Modern culture portrays the body as an object from which one can take pleasure, sometimes and sadly at the expense of another. John Paul II's response to this cultural co-modification of the body is this: "The body can never be an object for use. The body is sacred, it reveals the person and a person is a subject that can never be used, the only appropriate response to the person ever, is love."

Right from the beginning of time we are created for relationship with others, to love and to be loved in return. John Paul II reminds us that we cannot find meaning or purpose without loving relationships. While our culture would like to make sex the point in life, it often confuses sex and love.

John Paul II points out that before we are sexual beings, we are relational beings and that sex outside of relationship does not make sense, and without the context of relationship our body will not make sense either.

John Paul II describes the body as having a spousal or a nuptial attribute, which is the body's capacity for expressing love within a committed, covenant relationship of love between a man and a woman. This call to love, John Paul II says, is deeply inscribed within our bodily existence, as male and female, and is fully realized in the *"one flesh union"*.

When couples love each other they want to bless the other with a gift, to give a sign of their unconditional love. Within the one flesh union of marriage a husband and wife give and receive the body of the other. In making a gift of their body one to and for the other, they are saying, "this is my body which reveals the deepest part of who I am as a person, and I am giving myself to you...as a gift." It is a gift which is given unconditionally.

The nuptial meaning of the body is central to understanding *The Theology of the Body* as it refers to a man and woman's awareness of the deeply symbolic meaning of their physical bodies and their sexual actions; as gift. A gift which was designed by God, right from the beginning, to be a sign of his love.

"It (the body) includes right from the beginning the *nuptial* attribute, that is,
the capacity of expressing *love,* that love in which the
man-person becomes a gift and- by means of this gift-
fulfills the very
*meaning* of his existence."

{John Paul II}

Inscribed *deeply in the body,* is the ability and vocation to love, the greatest of the commandments.

*In the one flesh union the man and woman fully realize the call to become a gift for one another.*

*The very ability to make a gift of oneself in love is stamped into the very body of man and woman in the form of their sexuality.*

More important than understanding
the nuptial meaning of the body,
is the need to understand how it is
to be lived out,
for it is only in understanding
and living this out that the human
person will experience
*self-realization* and true *fulfillment.*

The *'nuptial meaning of the body'*
is characterized essentially by love,
*freedom* and the concept of gift.

"The revelation, and at the same time
the original discovery of the nuptial meaning of the body,
consists in this; it presents man, male and female, in the
*whole reality and truth* of his body and sex (they
were naked) and at the same time in full freedom from
any constraint of the body and of sex."

{John Paul II}

# The
# language of gift

We are called to speak a language with our body and that language is the language of the gift of love. This language of gift is in complete contradiction with modern day culture, which speaks the language of self, of using and taking to satisfy oneself. John Paul II describes this approach to the person as utilitarianism.

Nowhere more than in the sexual relationship is this language twisted and perverted to become the language of taking rather than giving.

Sadly, we live in a world that is totally misguided about the true meaning of love. Media and entertainment culture would have us believe that love is a feeling that we feel and the guiding force for our sexual decisions. We are all too familiar with the mantra...if it feels good...do it! While love is conveyed by feelings and emotions, love is confirmed by a decision to act, sometimes despite our feelings. Within marriage a couple may not always have loving feelings, but hopefully they will choose to act in a way that is loving, to make a gift of themselves in love. Love lies behind the loving feelings which we try to foster within a committed love- but feelings do not dictate love.

We are created by God with a desire for sexual union. There is nothing wrong with sexual desire and pleasure; it was created by God, and was created to be very good. This desire was granted as a gift to a husband and wife, for the purpose of helping them grow in their ability to make a sincere gift of themselves in love, one to and for the other. This desire for union and communion, within marriage, is a foreshadowing of the ultimate union that will at the end of time satisfy us completely, our relationship with God in heaven.

Virginity for the sake of the Kingdom is another way in which a person can live the truth of who they are as male or female, in seeking to make a sincere gift of their own self in love. This call to love in no way is a rejection of the desire for union and communion. Instead the person who commits themselves to virginity for the sake of the Kingdom, does so in anticipation of the ultimate union, that with God in heaven.

Marriage and virginity for the Kingdom are the two ways in which a person can fulfill their vocation, and in doing so, make manifest God's love here on earth. While marriage serves as an earthly sign of God's total free, faithful and fruitful love, virginity for the sake of the Kingdom is a sign of the ultimate marriage, the marriage of Christ and the Church.

The ultimate example of unconditional and sacrificial love was demonstrated by Jesus who gave his life for us on the cross. On our own it is impossible to live a life of sacrificial and self donative love but through the grace that is made available through Him we are able to love as Christ loves, which is the greatest commandment of all.

"This giving of oneself can only be achieved through the *freedom of the gift* which is rooted in the state of original nakedness.

It is in this state that man is able to love as God loves, by loving through his body, and in being a *gift* in this way he fulfills the very meaning of his existence."

{John Paul II}

"*Love is not merely a feeling,* it is an act of the will that consists of preferring, in a constant manner, the good of others to the good of oneself."

{John Paul II}

"Continence for the *kingdom of heaven* bears, above all, the imprint of the likeness of Christ. In the work of redemption, he himself made this choice for the kingdom of heaven."

{John Paul II}

"Virginity for the sake of the kingdom is a sign that the body whose end is not the grave, is directed towards *glorification.* Already by this very fact, continence for the kingdom of heaven is a witness among men that anticipates the future resurrection."

{John Paul II}

# Communio Personarum

-The ultimate love story-

One of John Paul II's most significant contributions to the Church's understanding of human sexuality and marriage is the development in his thought as to the specific manner in which we actually reflect the image and likeness of God. While the tradition long recognized that we reflect God through the faculties of intellect and free will, John Paul II taught that it is when we form a communion of persons -in the unity of two becoming one- that we most profoundly mirror God's image and likeness. This ability of two human persons to form a new and extraordinary community of love and relationship is referred to as the *communio personarum*- the community of persons.

The communion of persons in his teaching does not refer to a collection of people. It is not founded on common interest but rather the capacity the spouses possess to give of themselves; freely and, in turn, to receive the other, totally, faithfully and freely.

This capacity for total giving of self and receiving the other shares the dynamic of God's own love within the very heart of the Trinity. The Father, Son and Holy Spirit exist within a relationship of sacrificial and fruitful love, forming an eternal communion of persons.

The love of the Trinity is one of the greatest mysteries of our faith. So central is it to our lives that God designed us in such a way that we would be constantly reminded of this mystery.

Created in the image and likeness of God we are called to reveal and participate in the physical world the invisible mystery of God. It is in and through our bodies that we visibly make manifest this call to love. This is what John Paul II means when he speaks of the sacramentality of the body - a sacrament being that which makes visible in the physical world the invisible mystery of God, the mystery of the love that takes place within the Trinity, the love that gave itself on Calvary and a love that we are destined to share in both here on earth and in heaven.

John Paul II is very clear to point out that the body is a symbol, an icon, and does not bear an exact likeness to God. God is ineffable and eternal. However, the body is designed to direct us to something greater, "*to transfer into the visible world the invisible mystery of God.*"[2]

While the relationship that exists within the Trinity is not sexual, it is the sexual relationship between husband and wife that was designed, right from the beginning, to be a sacred sign and symbol of God's love within the Trinity here on earth. It is in this way that the body has a spousal or nuptial meaning and it is in understanding the body in this light that our relationships take on a deeper significance, meaning and potential.

"God has revealed his innermost secret:
God himself is an *eternal*
*exchange of love,* Father, Son and Holy Spirit,
and he has destined us to share in that exchange."

{Catechism}

*"Man was made in the image, not of the Father or the Son or the Spirit alone; but was made in the image of the Trinity"*

{Saint Augustine}

"*The body,* and it alone is capable of making visible what is invisible: *the spiritual and the divine.* It was created to transfer into the visible reality of the world the mystery hidden since time immemorial in God, and thus to be a sign of it."

{John Paul II}

"*Man and woman* are created individually in the image and likeness of God and are called to live in a *communion of love,* in this way they mirror to the world the image of God, that being the love that is expressed within the Trinity."

{John Paul II}

Marriage, being a *sacrament,* was
designed to make manifest God's love
here on earth; if we cannot see God's love
within the marital relationship here where
will we see it?

"In this entire world there is not a more perfect, more complete image of God, *Unity and Community* than marriage. There is no other human reality which corresponds more, humanly speaking to that divine mystery."

{John Paul II}

# THE HUMAN PERSON SERIES

*The Human Person Series* is a collection of books that seek to present some thoughts and reflections on the meaning of what it is to be a man and a woman in light of Pope John Paul II's work on the human person and human sexuality.

Based on Pope John Paul II's *Theology of the Body*, *The Human Person Series* presents busy men and women with the opportunity to reflect on the deeper meaning of their existence and their purpose in life.

 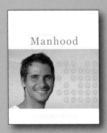 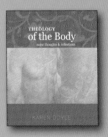

## www.thehumanperson.com

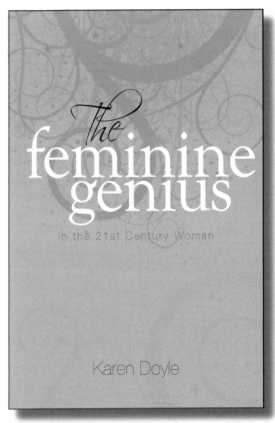

**COMING December 2008**

## Endnotes

1 John Paul II, *Theology of the Body,* Oct 22, 1980, (U.S.A, Daughters of St Paul) p164

2 John Paul II, *Theology of the Body,* Feb 20 1980, (U.S.A, Daughters of St Paul) p76.

CHOICEZ MEDIA is a rapidly growing and globally focused provider of values based sexuality seminars and resources. For more information on resources or to enquire about speaking engagements please visit the website:

www.choicez.com.au

---

Other resources from **CHOICEZ MEDIA**

## DVD FACILITATOR RESOURCES:

### *It's Your Choice*
A four part DVD program that looks at the pressures facing young people to be sexually active and encourages them to postpone sex until marriage.

### *The Problem with Pornography*
A three part DVD program for young men between 16-22 years of age, looking at the problem with pornography and encouraging toward a vision of manhood that values and respects women.

### *Things are Changing*
A puberty education package for parents and teachers working with young people.

### *LifeMatters Volume One*
A four part DVD program empowering young women to choose life giving options when faced with an unplanned pregnancy.

## AUDIO TEACHING CD'S:

Tips for parents
Tips for teachers
The rise of pornography